Healthy Soul

Faith Food Snack Pack

Faith Lifters that Bless and Build Believers

by
Nick Watson

Nick Watson Prophetic Power Ministries

youcanprophesy@gmail.com

www.youcanprophesy.com

Healthy Soul
Faith Food Snack Pack

ISBN 978-0-9943012-1-5

Copyright © by Nick Watson.

All rights reserved. No part of this book may be reproduced or transmitted in any form or by any means, electronic or mechanical, including photocopying and recording or by any information storage and retrieval system, without permission from the author.

Published by Nick Watson Prophetic Power Ministries.

Brisbane. Australia. 4178.

ENDORSEMENTS

Pastor Nick Watson broke new ground with his recent book, "You Can Prophesy – Supernatural. Simple. Safe." The book was straight forward, practical and releasing. His latest book is just as impacting and provides insight and wisdom which if applied will bring release to every person who reads it. As I read the book I was encouraged, inspired and motivated to apply the principles it espouses. I highly recommend you read the book and learn from Pastor Nick's personal understanding of profound scriptural principles.

Wayne Swift

National Leader, Apostolic Church Australia;
Senior Pastor, Church 1330. Scoresby. Victoria. Australia.

Firstly I loved it! – great revelation and content with strong Scriptural foundation and support evidenced right throughout the text. The chapters cover a good diversity of subjects with good use of simple illustrations. I like the application questions and Faith Declarations at the end of each chapter. For me as a preacher, it is certainly a great resource for messages, or preaching thoughts.

Gary Swenson

State Ministries Director,
Australian Christian Churches (previously Assemblies of God) Queensland and Northern Territory

Nick's book is full of great material and reads well. I'd describe it as a wonderful discipleship tool. I enjoy working through this sort of material with my staff team – it grows big people. Well done!!

Sheridyn Rogers

Senior Pastor, Network Leader, Activate churches, NZ

Nick Watson's new book lives up to its name! I found it very inspiring. You will find your faith lifted as you read each chapter. It is clear that he is not simply an author, but he has been a faithful pastor for decades. That pastoral grace comes through as Nick shepherds you into a stronger, more vibrant faith that works in every-day life. Enjoy reading Overcoming Faith Food Snack Pack as a solidly biblical and practical encouragement to strengthen your faith in Christ!

R. Sonny Misar

Author, "Journey to Authenticity". Senior Pastor, Living Light Church. Winona. Minnesota. USA

Nick's book is not only easy to read but one which is practical, has depth and encourages genuine discipleship. This book contains a good mix of Holy Ghost revelation, biblical fact and principles. This book poses simple yet effective principles of discipleship that will open our lives to God's favour and His anointing.

Chris Wickland

Senior Pastor, Living Word Church. Fareham. England.

As a minister of the Gospel for over 35 years I have learned to value good, sound teaching. So it is with pleasure that I recommend Nick Watson's new book. Nick is a seasoned prophet and pastor that understands the battles and trials we face daily and I believe his book will prove a blessing in practical teaching on overcoming these adversities of life.

Dr. Col Stringer

Author of 20 Christian books, President International Convention of Faith Ministers, Australia.

This book is a Biblical gold mine; written to inform truthfully and experientially its readers with life-changing Biblical principles for an exciting, fruitful, loving obedient, Christ-filled "Life!" Throughout the reading of this easy, comfortable, yet exciting writing style of Nick's, he keeps me turning the pages until I become time and again overcome by the wealth of confirmation and witness in my spirit of the treasure truths that are so beneficially needed in our lives at all times.

Rosemary Renninson

International Devotional Writer/Speaker. Moe. Vic. Australia

This is a book I enjoyed and will refer to again and again. For many years I have studied and taught pastoral ministry and done my best to be a good practitioner. This book would have been so helpful! Nick get this published and I will do my best to get it into as many hands I can.

Philip Underwood

Previously National Leader, Apostolic Churches, New Zealand; Senior Pastor (ret.) Cornerstone Church, Philadelphia. PA. USA

FOREWORD

Reading through this book, my heart rejoiced in the wisdom that came through the pages. This is a book of wisdom - and a gift to all believers, but particularly for those called to ministry. And I believe the Holy Spirit has inspired Nick to write this as an inheritance for the next generation of believers.

With many wonderful quotes and anecdotes, Nick imparts to us the blessing of many lessons learned through his years of ministry experience. There are many keys to be discovered by the reader about how to walk in wisdom. Prompting us with revelations and thought provoking stories, Nick has given us a gift that releases hope and help that, if applied, will cause you to walk in greater wisdom and favour.

One chapter had me "Amen-ing" aloud. Take time to absorb and apply the wonderful truths Nick has to share and you will be better for it!

Katherine Ruonala

Author of "Living in the Miraculous: How God's love is Expressed through the Supernatural"
Senior Leader of Glory City Church Brisbane and Apostolic oversight of the the International Glory City Church Network. Founder and Facilator of the Australian Prophetic Council.
www.katherineruonala.com

DEDICATION

My three dedications of this book are:

- To the Lord Who has partnered with me in many ways to write it.

- To my wife Lynne and our family of four generations.

- To the people who have encouraged me in ministry, so that I can pay-it-forward.

ACKNOWLEDGEMENTS

I thank my amazing wife and the love of my life, Lynne, for being my indispensable partner in life and in ministry.

My thanks also go to all those who have helped me put this book together. Firstly, my chief editor John MacFarlane without whose skills and efforts this book would not have come into reality. Secondly, my proof-reading family and friends Pastor Robert Couper, Elizabeth Scrimshaw, Barbara Hodgman, Lynne Watson and Bronwyn Cunningham.

Special mention and gratitude goes to Lisa Watson of the Printing Well, Wynnum for her sensational design of my book covers and other printing help she donated towards this project. *www.theprintingwell.com.au/*

AUTHOR'S CHOICE

I have made two non-traditional choices in this book. Firstly, I have deleted the definite article "the" from the Name of Holy Spirit, because I want Him to become more personal to my readers. Secondly, I have capitalised a lot of pronouns (such as "Him"), in order to give the Lord the honour He is due and to make clear Who the pronoun represents.

BIBLE QUOTATIONS

Unless stated otherwise, all Bible quotations in this book are taken from:

The Holy Bible, New International Version®, NIV® Copyright © 1973, 1978, 1984, 2011 by Biblica, Inc.® Used by permission. All rights reserved worldwide.

Other versions quoted:

King James Version. Public Domain.

The Amplified Bible. Zondervan Bible Publishers. © 1965. 24th reprinting – April, 1982

Scripture quotations marked ESV are from *The Holy Bible, English Standard Version®* (ESV®), copyright © 2001 by Crossway, a publishing ministry of Good News Publishers. Used by permission. All rights reserved.

Scriptures marked ISV are taken from the *Holy Bible: International Standard Version®*. Copyright © 1996-forever by The ISV Foundation. ALL RIGHTS RESERVED INTERNATIONALLY. Used by permission.

The Jerusalem Bible. DARTON, LONGMAN and TODD Ltd. And Doubleday and Company. London. 1968.

The Holy Bible, New Living Translation, copyright ©1996, 2004, 2007 by Tyndale House Foundation. Used by permission of Tyndale House Publishers, Inc., Carol Stream, Illinois 60188. All rights reserved.

The Living Bible copyright © 1971 by Tyndale House Foundation. Used by permission of Tyndale House Publishers Inc., Carol Stream, Illinois 60188. All rights reserved.

New American Standard Bible®, Copyright © 1960, 1962, 1963, 1968, 1971, 1972, 1973, 1975, 1977, 1995 by The Lockman Foundation Used by permission."

(www.Lockman.org)

New King James Version®. Copyright © 1982 by Thomas Nelson, Inc. Used by permission. All rights reserved."

Weymouth New Testament in Modern Speech. Third Edition 1913. (Public Domain).

Contents

Chapter 1 – You can be Strong 15

Chapter 2 God Who balances the Scales 31

Chapter 3 – Psalm 23 43

Chapter 4 – How to have a Healthy Soul: More like Jesus and More Joy 55

Chapter 5 – How to have a Healthy Soul: Train your Mind 65

Chapter 6 – How to have a Healthy Soul: Tame Your Tongue; Move On; Serve Others 77

Chapter 7 – Essential Christian Qualities: Love and Holiness 91

Chapter 8 – Essential Christian Qualities: Faith, Wisdom and Hope 101

Chapter 9 – 24-hour Prayer to Save a Multitude ... 111

INTRODUCTION

This mini-book is one of four taken from my book "Lessons from my Dog: 33 Faith-Lifters to bless and build believers." Each mini-book is a topical collection of life-transforming and equipping messages that cover a variety of subjects.

These are Holy Spirit inspired revelations, Biblical teachings, testimonies and illustrations that have proven fruitful in the lives of many people during my years as Senior Pastor of a thriving Spirit-filled, Apostolic church and travelling prophetic minister.

They will help you develop your God-given potential in Christ and equip you to fulfil your ministry that the Lord has assigned to you, by doing the good works of love and faith that He prepared in advance for you to do. (Ephesians 2:10).

I am honoured by the affirming comments of my anointed, experienced and internationally significant endorsers. Their reviews have confirmed to me that these books are going to meet needs, change lives, multiply ministry, equip believers and fulfil the purposes that the Lord entrusted to me when He anointed me as an author.

1 — *You can be* **Strong**

I can do all things through Christ Who strengthens me
Philippians 4:13

As you drive through a street you don't see much. How would you score if I pulled you over and asked you questions such as: "How many houses had red roofs? How many white fences did you see? Were there any dogs in the front yard? Which house had the biggest street number nailed on their fence?"

If you are like every other truthful driver, you would most likely say: "I think I would fail that test."

It's the same with the Bible. If you speed read your way through it, not much is going to sink in and you are going to miss some beautiful things that were there to inspire you.

I believe a close look at this one verse will prove this to you.

Before I focus on its specifics, let me say that you should bring your Bible to church and a pen so you can take notes. When you read your Bible at home or at work alone or on the train, write the thoughts you have about what you are reading in a notebook or even in your Bible itself.

Yes, I do mean scribble in your Bible.

On the other hand you can do as I do and take notes on your smartphone. It doubles as a Bible reader but I prefer to take a paper Bible with me.

Why don't you stop reading and stir your faith right now by saying out loud: "I can do all things through Christ Who strengthens me."

(i)   "I"

I want you to notice something about this verse – it is written in the singular, like Psalm 23. This verse is about each Christian's personal responsibility to partner with Jesus in his or her own life.

It is not written like the Our Father prayer Jesus taught His disciples, which is all plural. Jesus used all plurals to teach His disciples that believers should never pray selfish or self-centred prayers. We should always pray for others as well.

Holy Spirit's use of the singular pronouns in Philippians 4:13 tells us that each person must put his faith in the Lord to give him strength and victory. You can and you must trust the Lord Jesus to help you, in every area of life.

The "I" in this verse means that Christ will strengthen any and every Christian, without exceptions. That means you qualify for the Lord's help. Just put your name and your faith in this verse and Jesus will begin to give you His strength. Hallelujah.

(ii)   "I Can"

Christians must be positive people. You cannot have a negative mind and mouth and also say you have faith in God.

You cannot have a negative mind and mouth and also say you have faith in God.

Don't say "I can't", when God says "you can."

> *In your strength I can crush an army; I can run through a barricade; with my God I can scale any wall.*
> *Psalm 18:29*

Faith is real when you believe and act upon the principles and promises of God's Word. So by faith, act as if you can, not as if you can't.

(iii)   "Do"

The Bible says faith without works or actions is dead. So, I must act by faith, in accordance with God's Word.

If I feel afraid, I will act courageously because the Bible says "*God has not given me a spirit of fear.*" (2 Timothy 1:7).

If I need healing I will believe God to touch me with His power and demonstrate this by speaking out loud the Scriptures about healing and commanding my body to conform to the Word of God.

If my finances are tight, I faithfully and faith-fully implement Biblical economics by giving to God, sowing before I reap, acting wisely with my spending and working hard as unto the Lord. My active faith will trigger the Lord's help. I have heard plenty of testimonies over the years from Christians who have said at the end of a lean period: "The Lord got us through and provided for us every step along the way." I say Amen to that for myself and my family. Jehovah Jireh has brought us through every test and provided for us to not merely survive, but to be blessed in order to bless others.

Philippians 4:13 tells me that: I am the doer and Jesus is my power supply.

One of the greatest principles of faith in the Word of God is what the Lord said to Gideon.

> Then the LORD turned to him and said, "Go with the strength you have, and rescue Israel from the Midianites. I am sending you!"
> Judges 6:14

Don't wait until you have more strength or most likely until you "feel" you have more strength. Use the faith and the strength you already have. When you use what you've already got, Jesus will add His strength to it and you will triumph as Gideon did.

Here is another way to use your faith to plug into the strength of the Lord.

> ...Let the weak say, 'I am strong.'
> Joel 3:10b NKJV

(iv)   "All things"

Are these two words to be taken absolutely literally? No.

This verse does not mean a Christian can cook food without fire or fuel or power. It does not mean we can speak a foreign language without ever having learned it ... although I have heard of very rare miracles where this has happened.

Philippians 4:13 actually means that, through Christ, I can do all things that are God's Will for my life. Through Christ, I can do all the things God wants me to do.

- I can be a good father or mother
- I can be a good son or daughter
- I can be a good student
- I can be a good worker
- I can be a good minister for the glory of God
- I can be a good cook
- I can be a good on the computer
- I can be a good helper
- I can be a good example to others
- I can be a good leader
- I can be good in business
- I can be a good giver
- What do you need to be good at? Put it in here! "I can be a good ...."

God gives us the strength, resources and blessing to do all the things that He has willed for our lives.

You have probably heard the saying: "God's Will is God's bill." That is not just about money. It includes every resource you need to succeed in every area of life and ministry.

(v) "Through Christ"

The Greek word used here literally means "in Christ."

This tells us that we are not alone and we are not restricted to our human resources or limitations. We have a wonderful and powerful Partner, the Lord Jesus Christ Himself.

> *For out of His fullness (abundance) we have all received [all had a share and we were all supplied with] one grace after another and spiritual blessing upon spiritual blessing and even favour upon favour and gift [heaped] upon gift.*
>
> *John 1:16 AMP*
>
> *May you experience the love of Christ, though it is too great to understand fully. Then you will be made complete with all the fullness of life and power that comes from God.*
>
> *Ephesians 3:19 NLT*

Why don't you stop reading and say out loud right now: I am the doer and Jesus is my power supply.

Now speak out loud the Amplified Bible's version of Philippians 4:13.

> *I have strength for all things in Christ Who empowers me [I am ready for anything and equal to anything through Him Who infuses inner strength into me; I am self-sufficient in Christ's sufficiency].*

When you truly believe that Jesus really is in your life and you are truly in His, then all things will be possible to you.

Let's remind ourselves of the fact that Jesus lives within.

Right now, put your hand out in front of you as if you were about to shake another person's hand in greeting.

Because Jesus lives inside you, when you put out your hand, then He puts out His hand.

You are the Hands of Jesus now.

And that's not all.

- When Jesus wants to talk to someone He talks through you.
- When Jesus wants to touch someone He touches them through you.
- When Jesus wants to go somewhere, He goes there through you.

- When Jesus wants to love someone, He loves them through you.
- When Jesus wants to help someone, He helps them through you.

Our strength is not in ourselves, our personality, our talents, or our abilities. Our strength is not even our anointings or spiritual gifts. Our strength in our relationship with Jesus Christ, Who strengthens us.

> *Not that we are fit (qualified and sufficient in ability) of ourselves ......, but our power and ability and sufficiency are from God.*
> *2 Corinthians 3:5 AMP*

(vi)   "Strengthens"

I want you to notice that the word "strengthens" is in the present tense. It signifies that the Lord Jesus, Who is in you, is strengthening you in the very moment that you need His strength. In fact, Christ is continually strengthening you. You just need to be aware of His constant infilling and receive it by faith.

The present tense indicates that Jesus is continually able to pour in to us the power we need to succeed each and every day and moment. That continuing strength comes from a limitless Source. It flows into our lives, as we walk by faith in Christ and with Christ.

So, if we experience a "power shortage" or "power failure", it is not because of a failure in the supply from the Source. It is because of a failure to depend on and draw from the Source, by faith.

Any lack of strength is not because of a problem with Jesus the power-Supplier. We simply must learn how to draw from Him, our Source, by faith.

If you are about to do something difficult, say in your heart: "Lord, I draw on Your strength right now. I confess that I can do this because You are strengthening me in the here and now of my life. Amen."

(vii) "Me"

In English, Philippians 4:13 finishes with the same person it began with, namely, me.

There is a well-known saying: If it is to be – it's up to me

This verse tells each and everyone of us that we as individual believers must be in partnership with

Jesus in order to have the strength to fulfil all the things that the Lord has planned for us.

I cannot depend on or blame others. God plus me is enough to fulfil my potential and destiny. He will gather around me and unto me all the resources of people, money, things, opportunities, anointings, natural and spiritual gifts I need to succeed .... if I believe ... and if I act on what I believe about God and His Word.

If and when I become the doer, then Jesus will surely be my power-Supplier.

Even so faith, if it has no works, is dead ...
James 2:17 NAS

Here is a summary of what primary issues this verse addresses:

"I can" is about my Attitude, my Philosophy of life and ministry.

"Do" refers to my Actions, my Personal sense of responsibility.

"All Things" covers my Assignment, my Purpose.

"Through" and "in" Christ describes my Anointing, my Power-source.

"Strengthens" focusses on my Ability, my Potential in life and ministry.

Healthy Soul: Faith Food Snack Pack

Let's end this chapter with faith and gratitude by saying this verse out loud. But this time, I want you to say it three times and insert your own name as you do:

- I (your name here) can do all things through Christ Who strengthens me. Hallelujah.
- I (your name here) can do all things through Christ Who strengthens me. Hallelujah.
- I (your name here) can do all things through Christ Who strengthens me. Hallelujah.

What is one thing you have learned from this teaching?

_____

What is one thing you can do to implement this teaching?

_____

Faith Declaration:

I thank You Lord for strengthening me when I step out in faith. I praise you because Your Partnership in my life makes all things possible. I declare in Jesus' Name that I am not weak and I do not lack whatever it takes to succeed. I decree that I have strength for today, I have strength for every day, I have strength for every task, every situation and every opportunity, in Jesus' Name. Amen.

2. God Who balances the scales

A false balance is an abomination to the LORD, but a just weight is His delight.
Proverbs 11:1 NAS

The LORD detests double standards; He is not pleased by dishonest scales.
Proverbs 20:23

When we think of these verses in terms of life and not in a commercial context, we can see that the Lord is not pleased if our lives are out of balance. In this chapter, we learn from the prayer of Moses in Psalm 90 that we can ask and expect God to help us overcome life situations in which there is too much negativity and not enough good.

Give us gladness in proportion to our former misery! Replace the evil years with good.
Psalm 90:15

We all love a story about someone's rags-to-riches success, like that of Susan Boyle, runner-up on *"Britain's Got Talent"* in 2009.

We praise God for the testimony of a person who bounces back from adversity, like Bethany Hamilton. At the age of 13, she could have died when a shark attacked her. She lost her left arm. Her faith in God and personal determination were so strong that two years later she won first place in the Explorer Women's division of the USA National Scholastic Surfing Association Championships. Her story is told in the 2011 movie *"Soul Surfer"*. She certainly exemplifies the fact that having faith in God, Who balances the scales, will bring amazing turnarounds in your life.

Let's look at the second part of the little-known, but very encouraging, Psalm 90 verse by verse.

> [12] *Teach us to realise the brevity of life, so that we may grow in wisdom.*

Life has a way of seemingly slipping through our fingers. Children grow up so fast. I think our culture causes our children to grow up too fast. Parents should make sure their children are not being exposed to knowledge and experiences that they are not mature enough to process positively.

Understanding that life is brief, like a fog that lifts and dissipates quickly after it has formed (refer James 4:14), is an important motivator to living a focussed, purposeful life. That is one way a person can live a wise life. They will make the best they can of the life they have.

The greatest priority that should be evoked by understanding how brief is our earthly life, is that we live with eternity in mind. That means living God's way, not man's way, not our own way. It means living for His glory and His reward, not for the glory of man, or self, or the rewards of this worldly life. This is one of the meanings of Proverbs 9:10 which says: *"the fear of the Lord is the beginning of wisdom."*

When you live with eternity as your focus, you understand that there will be a day of judgement for each and every human being, on the day of the Lord's choosing. That's a good reason to live wisely, meaning with godly wisdom. It's a good reason to live a life based on the Bible and to make Jesus your Saviour and Lord.

Another aspect to realising the brevity of life is to understand that if your life is to turn around, as this prayer is asking God to do, you must learn from the mistakes of the past. Don't waste time living in the past. Don't let the past imprison you.

> [13] *O LORD, come back to us! How long will You delay? Take pity on Your servants!*

If you want your life to turn around, you must get right with God. Imagine having a shirt with a full row of buttons down the front. If you get the first button wrong, then every other button is out of sync and you look completely out of order. That's what life is like when you don't put God first in your life. Your life is not in the order or balance God desires. This will frustrate both you and the Lord, either in the short or long term or both.

The Great Shepherd Psalm (23) promises that goodness and mercy will follow those who follow Jesus, like good sheep of His pasture. If they don't follow Him, this and all the other promises of that extraordinary Psalm do not apply. Moses' prayer recognises that a person must be in good relationship with God if they want their life to be better than it has been.

> [14] *Satisfy us each morning with your unfailing love, so we may sing for joy to the end of our lives.*

Knowing the love of God in a personal way has tremendous comforting, healing, uplifting and esteem-building side-effects. In the otherwise quite miserable book of Lamentations there is a bright, shining jewel of light and hope:

God Who Balances the Scales

^{22} The faithful love of the Lord never ends! His mercies never cease. ^{23} Great is His faithfulness; His mercies begin afresh each morning. ^{24} I say to myself, "The Lord is my inheritance; therefore, I will hope in Him!"

Lamentations 3:22-24 NLT

This tells us that no matter how dark, lonely or depressing your life might be at this time, God can always touch you with His love, refresh you with His mercy and give you hope for the future. The Lord is your inheritance. God has a rich inheritance of all the promises in His Word for you to experience and enjoy.

His new mercy, new grace, new love, new blessing, new hope, new peace and new power are yours for the taking, by faith, each and every day. Whether you had a good day or a bad one yesterday or the day before or for however long, you can start each new day believing for a better day today. When you believe, you will receive the resources you need from the Lord to achieve success.

You can start each new day believing for a better day today. When you believe, you will receive the resources you need from the Lord to achieve success.

> ¹⁵ *Give us gladness in proportion to our former misery! Replace the evil years with good.*

This is the big thing for which you can hope. This is what you can believe God will do for you. If you can have this kind of faith in the God Who balances the scales of your life, then you can experience the reverse of what Egypt did. Based on the interpretation of Pharoah's dreams, Joseph predicted that seven good years of prosperity would be followed by seven years of drought leading to an international famine.

This prayer believes for the Lord to put His hand of favour, blessing, provision and power on your life for years to come. This will well and truly reverse the curse of sin and Satanic opposition and fleshly stupidity that have depleted your life.

¹⁶ *Let us, your servants, see You work again; let our children see Your glory.*

Now Moses prays for the evident power and glory of God to be revealed to His people and their families. What a magnificent experience it is to have a Divine encounter with the manifest presence of God. How marvellous it is when God Himself "shows up" in worship or empowers a person to get out of their wheelchair completely healed and able to live a normal life again. This is what Moses is encouraging us to pray for.

Yes, God is omnipresent. He is present everywhere, all the time. However, we humans do not see Him or feel Him everywhere, all the time. We know He is there by faith. We know He is there, with us, as God, the Omnipresent, Omniscient, Omnipotent covenant-keeping Senior Partner of His people. The Book of Esther testifies that God still does supernatural things while remaining invisible. It also teaches us that God is at work even we don't realise it or see anything happening.

The Book of Esther testifies that God still does supernatural things while remaining invisible. It also teaches us that God is at work even we don't realise it or see anything happening.

When the Lord chooses to reveal Himself in an obvious way, it is a special moment indeed. This is what we want our families to experience. This is what makes God so very real and personal to them as individuals. This is why it is so rare for people saved during a genuine revival to ever waiver in their faith. It's because they have had a personal encounter with the Living God. Hallelujah. `

I think it is fair to say that God has been revealing Himself more and more in recent decades, through visions, dreams and manifestations of His supernatural knowledge and power. There also seem to be far more revelations of angels in an ongoing fulfilment of what Jesus said to Nathaniel in John 1:51.

> [17] *And may the Lord our God show us his approval and make our efforts successful. Yes, make our efforts successful!*

Now Moses demonstrates the requirement for our active faith, not just faith in prayer. God does not just do things for us. He works with us to make our works of love, faith and obedience successful. You can be sure that when the Lord is truly your personal Senior Partner, He will make your efforts successful as He did for Joseph and David in the Old Testament. (Genesis 39:2-3; 1 Samuel 18:14).

We receive all things the same way we receive salvation. Ephesians 2:8 tells us that we are saved by grace through faith. Every good thing we get from God is because of His unconditional generosity toward His children. However, receiving what God gives requires our obedient, active faith.

Keep on asking, and you will receive what you ask for.

Matthew 7:7 NLT

When Jesus made this statement He used two strong words. When you study the word Jesus used for "ask", you discover that it has the implicit meaning of putting a demand on the grace of God based on a covenant, the requirements of which have been met. Of course, He said this before He met those requirements; but because of Calvary, the new covenant has been sealed and activated by Jesus' sacrifice and triumph.

The word Jesus used for "receive" is the Greek word "lambano". This is another strong word. It has military connotations, because it means to "seize". So, receiving is not a passive thing. Some Christians think that, if they pray sometimes and go to church occasionally and even read their Bibles every now and then, God should shower them with blessings while they are watching television or when they are in need.

Jesus used a strong word for "receive". "Lambano" means to "seize". Receiving is not a passive thing.

The reality is that God responds more to faith than He does to need. Hebrews 11:6 says the Lord rewards those who *"earnestly seek Him."* (NIV). Those who receive blessings and miracles the "lambano" way are those who put their faith on the line consistently, as a lifestyle and specifically in regard to the particular blessings and miracles they are seeking.

For example, they sow financially, when they are believing for financial breakthrough, because the Bible says first give, then second it will be given to you. (Luke 6:38). Similarly, they confess the word of God for their healing while they are trusting God for their bodies to become well.

So, if you want the prayer of Moses, recorded in Psalm 90, to become real in your life, you will need to be consistent and persistent in active faith, appropriate to the specific blessings and miracles you are trusting God to manifest in your life, according to His Word.

What is one thing you have learned from this teaching?

What is one thing you can do to implement this teaching?

Faith Declaration:

I thank You Lord that You are my God, Who puts Your hands of favour and power on the scales of my life to give me success as I live and work by faith, to turn my loss and pain into gain, my mourning into dancing, my frustration into fulfilment, my sickness into health, my poverty into wealth and my depression into joy. I entrust my life to You afresh and prophesy by faith that today will be a good day for me and my family. I step into Your good plans for my life, family, vocation, ministry and future, in Jesus' Name. Amen. I ask and believe You Lord to reveal Yourself to every member of my family and to let everyone around us see Your good and great hand upon us, for Your own glory's sake. Amen.

3   Psalm 23

The Lord is my Shepherd [to feed, guide, and shield me], I shall not lack.

Psalm 23:1 AMP

This is an intensely personal Psalm. That makes it quite different from the Lord's Prayer, which is written entirely in the plural. By doing that, Jesus was subtly teaching us we should not be selfish in prayer but always include others.

The Bible tells us that we cannot change what is written in Scripture in any way. (refer Galatians 1:9 & 5:7-10; Revelation 22:18-19). However, I like to add a word at the beginning of this first verse in order to clarify that the wonderful promises throughout Psalm 23 are conditional, not automatic. The word is "when". So let me take the risk of adding that word to the start of verse one.

When the Lord is my shepherd, I shall not want …… and (going all the way to the end verse 6) …… goodness and mercy will follow me all the days of my life.

Now imagine you are being a good sheep of the Lord. You are following the Lord and goodness and mercy are following you. All four of you are walking around in a line, one behind the other. If Jesus turns left, so do you and so do goodness and mercy. If Jesus turns right, so do you and so do goodness and mercy.

What happens if Jesus turns left and you turn right? Let me assure you that goodness and mercy will turn left, because, really, they follow Him, not you. They only follow you, when you follow Him. If you step out of line with the Lord, your Shepherd, then you won't be in the right position to receive all the benefits, blessings and resources He was leading you to.

Goodness and Mercy and all the benefits of Psalm 23 actually follow Jesus, not you. If you follow Him, they will follow you.

Jesus gives Rest and Peace

> *He makes me lie down in [fresh, tender] green pastures; He leads me beside the still and restful waters.*
>
> *Psalm 23:2 AMP*

The Lord knows how to care for his flock, so they are healthy sheep. He provides all we need to succeed. This is the real meaning of this verse and the verse in the "Our Father" prayer: "Give us this day our daily bread."

If more people in this stressful, hectic Western world we live in, would let Jesus be their Lord and Shepherd, they would experience so much more peace and rest and refreshing times in their lives. Jesus Himself reinforced this promise in Matthew 11:28-30.

Jesus heals within

> *He restores my soul; He guides me in the paths of righteousness for His name's sake.*
> *Psalm 23:3 NAS*

This is an outstanding promise. When the Lord is your shepherd, He will repair your inner being. Just as Jesus went back to heaven bearing scars, as did the apostle Paul (according to Galatians 6:17), so do we. In Western Christianity, our scars tend to be internal rather than physical. This is one reason we used this saying as the motto of our children's ministry. "It is better to build children than repair adults."

> *Even though I walk through the valley of the shadow of death, I fear no evil, for You are with me; Your rod and Your staff, they comfort me.*
>
> *Psalm 23:4*

This great verse is often read at funerals, because the shadow of a loved one's death has come over his or her family and friends.

It is an example of some of the negative things we have inside that the Lord can heal, things like grief, regret and guilt. I remember doing a funeral for a father who died suddenly in a work accident in another country. His sixteen year old daughter was distraught because the last interaction she had with her dad, before he went away, was a bad one.

On one such occasion, the Lord said to me concerning a Christian who had died and the Christian family he left behind: "I will stand in the gap in the lives of those left behind for the one who has gone to eternity." What a wonderful promise that is.

Valleys are tough on both the way down and the way up. We need the Lord with us, whatever direction we are travelling. We also need other people, just as mountain climbers do. Don't be so super-spiritual that you do not recognise your need for God when He has skin on. The Lord normally works through people, as well as doing things Himself.

When you know the Lord is with you, your faith chokes out your fear. You have a greater peace and confidence no matter what the circumstances of your life are, when you have a well-developed personal love relationship and faith partnership with Jesus.

The shepherd's staff was to lovingly keep the sheep in line and rescue them from any slips they made. The rod was a weapon against the enemies of the flock. How encouraging it is to know that the Lord is always ready to pick us up when we fall down. He is also there with us to not only defend us from any attacks we suffer, but to prevent us from being attacked and to bring restoration to our lives for any losses we incur.

Jesus provides for us, regardless of our difficulties

> *You prepare a feast for me in the presence of my enemies. You honour me by anointing my head with oil. My cup overflows with blessings.*
>
> *Psalm 23:5 NLT*

How great is our God. The fact that we have enemies arrayed against us cannot prevent the Lord getting His abundant blessings and resources through to us.

So when you are faced, not with Hittites, Amalekites and Canaanites as the ancient Israelites were, but with Bill-ites, Sick-ites, Stress-ites and the like, you have an omnipotent Lord and master Shepherd Who can still provide you with all you need and, according to 2 Corinthians 9: 8, enough to share.

That is talking about external adversities such as an economic downturn or the lack of co-operation of key people in our lives. The second part of this verse refers to internal issues that can hinder us from receiving God's provision.

God wants us to have an overflowing cup. Notice the order recorded here. A Christian's head has to be anointed with oil before, by faith, they move into the abundance of grace that God has for them.

Your mind needs to be renewed with God's oil, meaning by His Spirit and according to His Word, before you will experience and overflowing life.

This is what Israel needed before they defeated their foes in the Promised Land. They had to have a positive mind-set before they went to war. That's why the Lord removed the reproach from them before they began to possess the land God had given them. (Joshua 5:9).

According to Joshua 5:2-8, the army of Israel was circumcised after they crossed the Jordan. In a brilliant display of the Lord's protection in a time of vulnerability, they were not attacked by their nearby enemy, who knew the Israelites were there, during their time of healing.

You can ask God for that kind of protection too. I have sometimes cried out to the Lord, saying: "Don't let any more negativity or pressure touch my life or family or church right now, because we are at our limits and very vulnerable." God has been faithful to me by never allowing me to be tempted more than I can bear. (1 Corinthians 10:13).

The Lord will protect you in your times of vulnerability. Ask Him to do this for you.

> Then the LORD said to Joshua, "Today I have rolled away the shame of your slavery in Egypt." So that place has been called Gilgal to this day.
>
> Joshua 5:9 NLT

God did a transformation for the Jews when they got circumcised. Their shame was rolled away. Their slave mentality, their poverty spirit and other such negative mental attitudes and emotional baggage was removed from them. Their past could no longer sabotage or limit their future.

This is what renewing your mind does. When your head is anointed with the oil of the Spirit and washed with the water of the Word of God, your soul is healed, your mind is transformed. This makes you ready to believe for and embrace the victories and abundant grace that the Lord has prepared for you. Hallelujah.

Jesus provides good things for you in life and in Heaven forever

> *Surely goodness and mercy shall follow me all the days of my life; And I will dwell in the house of the LORD forever.*
>
> *Psalm 23:6*

Here's the beautiful thing about having faith in God: you get to taste and see that the Lord is good on earth and in Heaven forever. There's nothing better than that.

Psalm 27 says something that is so very encouraging. It starts with the Psalmist declaring that he will be "confident", regardless of how many enemies are arrayed against him. He declares that his relationship with God is his highest priority and the key to his victory.

In verse 10 he says that even if his parents forsook him, he believed the Lord would pick him up and take care of him. His faith enables him to be confident of something else: *"I will see the goodness of the Lord in the land of the living."* (verse 13).

My point is this: the final verse of Psalm 23 tells us that, when the Lord is our shepherd, we can expect God's favour, provision, love, protection, mercy and goodness in this life, as well as every infinitely good thing in Heaven forever.

With Jesus, it's not just pie in the sky when you die, it's steak on your plate while you wait. Hallelujah!

With Jesus, it's not just pie in the sky when you die, it's steak on your plate while you wait. Hallelujah!

If there is one simple truth you should gain from Psalm 23, it is like a coin a two-sided one. The first side is that Jesus is the most amazing Shepherd anyone could ever have. He will take care of you and provide for you, no matter what happens in your life, nor who else helps you or lets you down.

The second side is that you need to be a good sheep. Love the Lord. Let Him lead you. Trust Him and turn to Him for the resources you need to survive the worst of times, to be sustained in the ordinary and testing times of life and to succeed in both being who you are meant to be and doing what you are called to do through all the times of your life and ministry.

Psalm 23

What is one thing you have learned from this teaching?

What is one thing you can do to implement this teaching?

Faith Declaration:

I thank You Lord for all the wonderful promises of Psalm 23 that You have given to me from the moment of my salvation and submission to Jesus as my Saviour, Shepherd and Lord. I am grateful that You help me get through the valley experiences in my life. I praise You as my Provider and Peace-Giver. I rejoice in You, because my enemies cannot prevent You from resourcing me with anointing oil and an overflowing cup. I am grateful for Your goodness, mercy and loving-kindness following me, as I follow You. I give You praise for making me welcome in Heaven and for preparing a place there for me in Your Father's House. Amen.

How to have a Healthy Soul: *More like Jesus and More Joy*

Dear friend, I am praying that all is well with you and that your body is as healthy as I know your soul is.

3 John 2 NLT

Beloved, I pray that you may prosper in every way and [that your body] may keep well, even as [I know] your soul keeps well and prospers.

3 John 2 AMP

The actual Greek word used by John can be translated as meaning "to have a prosperous journey", or, in other words "to succeed". This translation pictures a person being successful because they are on the right track.

The word "all" means the believer can prosper in every area of life, including spiritually, in family life and all relationships, in ministry, business or career, in finances, in education and in social activities they enjoy.

The apostle John is praying that his dear friend will be as successful in his finances and career and destiny and relationships and bodily health as he is in his inner health. The inner-world health of his spiritual life and of his soul, his mind-will-and-emotions, are important to his physical and outer-world success.

John must have known nearly 2,000 years ago, what is still observable today. Often, the sickness and poverty of a person's soul (i) prevents them from enjoying God and life; (ii) opens the way for sickness to attack their body; and (iii) hinders them from fulfilling their true potential and destiny in Christ.

I want to point out two things about this simple but powerful prayer. Firstly, although it is John's, the very fact that Holy Spirit included it in his epistle means that the Lord intended for us to benefit from it. John was praying from his heart, but his heart was so in tune with God's that his prayer was the same as what the Lord would have prayed.

Secondly, and this is rather obvious, the prayer is a dangerous one. If your soul is not prospering, this prayer works in the negative as well as the positive. Unhealthiness in our soul creates blockages to our faith and to the helping and healing power of Holy Spirit.

Years ago there was a Christian movie called "The Flywheel." Before the central character comes to the Lord in full discipleship commitment, he sells a car to his pastor for an exorbitant price. Before he leaves the pastor's home with his cash, the pastor prays for him. It went something like this: "Lord bless him, as he has blessed me today." The salesman went home with plenty to think about. Maybe he prayed: "Lord, please don't answer my pastor's prayer." You don't have to be the smartest Christian in town to guess which of those two prayers the Lord would answer. I hope you treat your pastor better than that.

In this and the next chapter I will show you six ways by which you can develop a healthier soul.

(i)   Become more like Jesus (Romans 8:29)

We become more like Jesus by growing the fruit of the Spirit. (Galatians 5:22–23a). Obviously, the name of this fruit tells us that Holy Spirit helps us grow in this way. However, He doesn't do it for us. We have to use our faith to make such character transformations as replacing anger with peace and depression with joy.

Here is a beautiful and powerful promise we can believe God for and see worked out progressively in our lives: Whatever is not right within you can be changed by the Lord your Shepherd Who restores your soul. (Psalm 23:3a).

Remember, the fruit of the Spirit is not limited to the nine well-known characteristics listed in Galatians. Other Christ-like fruit we develop as we mature in the things of God include holiness, mercy, empathy, generosity, humility, wisdom, courage and servanthood.

> *The merciful man does good for his own soul, But he who is cruel troubles his own flesh.*
> *Proverbs 11:17 NKJV*

When you keep your eyes on Jesus, not on people or incidents or circumstances, your heart will stay healthy. As you continue to behold Him, you will be changed. (2 Corinthians 3:18).

(ii)   Make room for Joy in your life

We need to cultivate joy in our lives. We have to intentionalise how to experience more joy and then schedule happy times.

In recent years laughing clubs have multiplied around the world. People have found that as they choose to laugh out loud, in company with others who are simultaneously doing the same, their mind-generated laughing becomes as infectious and gratifying as spontaneous laughter. Their mental choice affects their feelings.

I know some Spirit-filled ministers who have done the same, alone in their home or car, in order to cultivate more joy in their lives. I haven't tried it yet.

> A cheerful heart is good medicine, but a crushed spirit dries up the bones
> *Proverbs 17:22*

This verse tells us that our attitudes and emotions, in other words our inner health, have an impact on our physical health. Improving the condition of our soul contributes positively to our receiving Divine healing.

The margin of the New American Standard Bible says that a joyful heart "literally, 'causes good healing.'" In other words, even the Bible recognises that there is a direct, cause-and-effect process: a merry heart produces good healing. Conversely, a broken or crushed spirit has a negative effect on our health (it "dries up the bones").

The state of our soul can certainly and substantially affect our good health or contribute to our lack of it.

Healthy Soul: Faith Food Snack Pack

Doctors sometimes diagnose illnesses as being psychosomatic in origin. This scientific word comes from the same Greek words that the Bible uses for "soul" (the psyche) and "body" (the soma).

Some doctors refuse to acknowledge a miracle when the evidence of one is clearly and irrefutably presented to them. However, the medical world does agree with the Bible and the prayer of the apostle John on this subject, namely, that the state of our inner being can substantially affect our outward physical health, for good or for bad.

Let me give you two specific examples to consider.

> *Men's hearts failing them for fear....*
> *Luke 21:26 KJV*

Is it possible that this is literally true? I think you could easily find many doctors who would agree that people have heart attacks which are triggered by fear.

Secondly, consider the following Scriptures that seem to indicate there is a relationship between grief and poor eyesight. Could this be literally true? I think it could. Psalm 6:7; Psalm 88:9.

> *My eye has grown dim because of grief, and all my members are [wasted away] like a shadow.*
> *Job 17:7*

Notice the second half of this verse in the book of Job introduces a third example of a psychosomatic link, namely, between grief and depression and weight loss. I believe there is such a link. I also know that, for many people depression is a source of weight gain, as they "comfort-eat". They eat not because they are hungry, but somehow eating gives them an up-lift. Unfortunately, like a lot of self-medicated quick fixes, overeating has serious, negative long-term consequences, including depression.

Jesus made it clear that He wants us to experience His joy. (John 16:24; 17:13)

> *These things I have spoken to you so that My joy may be in you, and that your joy may be made full.*
> *John 15:11 NAS*

Joy is one of the fruit of the Spirit in Galatians 5:22. So, as Christians mature in Christ-likeness, they should have more joy. Jesus does not want believers to go around as if they had been baptised in lemon juice. We will have both serious and sad times in life, but that should not exclude regular doses of joy.

All the fruit of the Spirit have to be grown deliberately. We are not all automatically endowed with qualities such as patience, long-suffering and kindness. Even God's kind of agape-love, which is described in 1 Corinthians 13:4-8a, doesn't just grow naturally. It is something we need to develop.

Joy is the same as those other fruit of the Spirit. It requires deliberate cultivation on our behalf in order to grow.

Schedule some fun things in your life. Learn to relax. Live your life according to your own priorities, not someone else's agenda. I learned a long time ago that I cannot be in two places at once. So, I can say no to certain demands on my life, in order to do something I need or even want to do without feeling guilty about it.

For your own health's sake, regularly do some things that make you happy. It might be spending time with your family or playing sport or going to a movie or doing a hobby. If all else fails, get a puppy!

It is unhealthy and not at all good for your joy-tank to spend too much time alone, even if you are playing your favourite game on your laptop or X-box. Some solitude is good for us, but loneliness leads to depression.

When you are alone, spend quality time with God. Count your blessings. Give Him thanks for the good things in your life. Dream of better days ahead as you walk by faith into the good plans the Lord has for you. (Jeremiah 29:11).

What is one thing you have learned from this teaching?

_____

What is one thing you can do to implement this teaching?

_____

Faith Declaration:
I thank You Lord for empowering me, by Your Word and Holy Spirit to become more like Jesus. Like John the Baptist, I say let Him increase in me, so people see more of Jesus through me. I declare that I am maturing in Christ and that all the fruit of the Spirit will be seen in my life. I thank You Lord for greater joy in my life today and in my future, in Jesus' Name. Amen.

5

How to have a Healthy Soul:
Train your Mind

Dear friend, I pray that you may enjoy good health and that all may go well with you, even as your soul is getting along well.

3 John 2 NIV

Beloved, I pray that you may prosper in all things and be in health, just as your soul prospers.

3 John 2 NKJV

In the previous chapter, I described two ways you can cultivate a healthy soul, namely, by becoming more like Jesus and by cultivating more joy in your life. In this chapter, I will outline a third way, which is the training of your mind.

Renewing your mind leads you into your destiny.

> *Don't copy the behaviour and customs of this world, but let God transform you into a new person by changing the way you think. Then you will learn to know God's will for you, which is good and pleasing and perfect.*
>
> *Romans 12:2 NLT*

David knew this pattern and result when, under the inspiration of Holy Spirit, he wrote in Psalm 23 verse 5 that first your head has to be anointed with oil and then second your cup will overflow.

When a person becomes a Christian, their spirit comes alive, but their soul and body do not automatically change one hundred percent to demonstrate that they are now Christians. The renewing of our minds is essential to becoming more like Christ, because no-one automatically thinks, speaks, acts or reacts the way God wants us to. We must all learn how to live Christianly. We do this by changing our thoughts, words and actions to be led by Holy Spirit and in accordance with the Word of God so that we think Biblically, Christianly and positively at all times.

When your mind is renewed, you are changed and you begin to walk in the true will of God for your life. According to Romans 12:2, that Divine Will is good for you, acceptable to you and perfect for you.

Therefore, you enjoy your life more and you do better in every sphere of life.

Renewing your mind improves your quality if life

As the Word of God renews our mind it also restores and refreshes our soul, it brings us life and radiant health, it imparts Godly wisdom to us and it lifts us spiritually, by boosting our faith.

> *The law of the LORD is perfect, restoring the soul; the testimony of the LORD is sure, making wise the simple.*
> *Psalm 19:7 NAS*

> *Pay attention, my child, to what I say. Listen carefully. [21]Don't lose sight of my words. Let them penetrate deep within your heart, [22]for they bring life and radiant health to anyone who discovers their meaning.*
> *Proverbs 4:20-22 NLT*

> *So then faith comes by hearing, and hearing by the word of God.*
> *Romans 10:17 NKJ*

The fact of life is that we are bombarded by so much negativity on a daily basis. It infiltrates our soul, just as grass and dust attach to our body when we mow the lawn.

Bad things that happen to us affect the way we think. It would be great if negative things only affected us in a small way and positive things in a big way. Sadly, all too often, for too many people, it is the opposite of that.

Bad things seem to hit like a hurricane or a bullet even if they are only small and we remember them for a long time. By contrast, we enjoy the moment, but so quickly and easily forget good things after they occur.

Even small, bad things can hit hard and impact us, and we quickly and easily forget good things.

Renewing your mind is like learning a new language

The New Testament talks about renewing our minds, our attitudes, the way we think, because the

Lord knows how big a task it is to overcome the implanted teachings of the world and become a person who thinks Biblically, having the Mind of Christ. It's as hard as learning a new language.

The other reason it's like learning a new language is that renewing your mind requires you to renew your mouth. As you change your mind, you change the way you speak .... and vice versa.

Renewing your mind requires you to renew your mouth. As you change your mind, you change the way you speak .... and vice versa.

I am not very good at distinguishing tones in music. For me to learn a tonal language like Chinese would be a lifelong learning experience that I would have to seriously dedicate myself to mastering.

It takes serious commitment to renew your mind with the Word of God. Ephesians 4:22-24 gives us a 3-step pattern to follow:

Firstly, put off your old self – in the words of 2 Corinthians 10:5 "take captive every thought to make it obedient to Christ".

Secondly, be made new in the attitude of your mind.

Thirdly, put on the new self, which I translate, for the purpose of this teaching, as meaning: put on the new mind. Let your thoughts be made like God's thoughts. Learn to think according to what the Bible says.

The rewards of renewing your mind

The rewards of renewing your mind are well worth it. As your mind and attitudes change for the better, your faith grows, you become a better person, you overcome things like depression, confusion and fear, you enjoy your life more, your health gets better, your communication, relationships and your work performance all improve. In other words you begin to prosper in every area of your life, because the prayer of 3 John 2 is coming true for you.

A simple illustration of this is that even the medical profession acknowledges the healing power of good attitudes. The Bible puts it this way:

> *A merry heart does good like a medicine*
> *Proverbs 17:22 KJV*

I was not blessed by starting life as an optimist. It has taken me literally years of faith and years of absorbing God's Word, to develop a healthy soul and a positive mind-set.

One of the most important attitudes to adopt is that of living and functioning as a child of God under His New Covenant of Grace. I don't have to earn God's love or favour. I don't have to perform in a certain way at a required level to get anything from God. All has been given to me freely by grace, because of what Jesus did for me before, on and after the Cross.

Renewing your mind takes deliberate, consistent effort

There is a reason why people talk about the battlefield of the mind. Firstly, your own worldly-educated, proud, rebellious, sin-loving mind does not want to give up control of your life to the Lord. So you have to conquer and crucify the enemy within.

Let me explain what step one in Ephesians 4:22 really means. You must not simply put off your old ways of thinking as you would a shirt that was dirty after wearing it for a day. You might have every intention of wearing it again another day.

Your stinking thinking has got to be put to death. Some thought patterns are so deeply ingrained they have to be put to death a thousand times, or maybe a thousand times a thousand times. You have to replace the old electro-chemical tracks in your brain with new ones built by the Word of God, with the help of Holy Spirit.

The second reason you will have a battle renewing your mind is because the devil will not cooperate with you as you seek to shut out his influences. They include lies, accusations, temptations, discouragements, depression, oppression, and condemnation. The devil knows that he will lose his control over you once you learn to consistently choose right, holy, positive thoughts and reject wrong, sinful, negative ones. Satan is a master at bombarding people's minds, both Christians and sinners, with negativity. You must resist him.

You have to learn how in Christ to wear the helmet of salvation to protect your thought life and how to lift up the shield of faith against every attack of the evil one and how to use the Word of God as your sword of truth and victory over the devil and his demons.

Through faith and persistence, the Lord will help you, to overcome bad mental habits. You will break free of controlling influences such as fear, anger, poverty, lust, greed, inferiority, inadequacy, depression and pride. You will live a new and better life.

Choose to have a positive mind, not a negative one

Look at the contrast these verses make between a negative mind and a positive one. Which would you choose? Which do you choose? Will you choose the right mind and the good fruit of it every day of your Christian life until it is a reality in your thinking, in your emotions and in your life?

> *All the days of the desponding and afflicted are made evil [by anxious thoughts and foreboding], but he who has a glad heart has a continual feast [regardless of circumstances].*
>
> *Proverbs 15:15 AMP*

> *Those who live according to the flesh have their minds set on what the flesh desires; but those who live in accordance with the Spirit have their minds set on what the Spirit desires. [6] The mind governed by the flesh is death, but the mind governed by the Spirit is life and peace.*
>
> *Romans 8:5-6*

There are some things we can learn from these verses.

(i)   If you have a problem with the negativity of your mind, don't just sit around all day, thinking too much.

(ii)   You cannot have a positive life, when you have a negative mind. Right thinking leads to victorious Christian living. Stinking thinking leads to mediocrity, negativity, frustration and failure. However, be aware of this: positive thoughts and positive words do not alone or automatically generate success. For example, you can think and speak positively about your career, but if you never apply for a job, you're not likely to get one.

You cannot have a positive life, when you have a negative mind.

(iii)   You have to set your mind on the right things. (Philippians 4:8). Positive thoughts are full of faith, hope, and love. Negative thoughts are full of fear, doubt, anger and unforgiveness.

God will and good people can help you reap the benefits of a renewed mind

Here is some good news for you. If you change the way you think, you will change who you are and what you do with your life.

> *For as (a man) thinks within himself, so he is...*
> *Proverbs 23:7a NAS*

You are not alone in this process. You can and should get the help you need from other Christians whose minds and lives have been transformed. You will also have the Lord's help.

> *God has not given us a spirit of timidity, cowardice ... and ... fear, but ... of power, and of love and of calm and well-balanced mind and discipline and self-control.*
> *2 Timothy 1:7 AMP*

It takes time and effort to retrain our minds, but the rewards are worth waiting and working for. God Himself will be with you to empower you in this positive change and personal growth process.

> *For I am confident of this very thing, that He who began a good work in you will perfect it until the day of Christ Jesus.*
> *Philippians 1:6*

What is one thing you have learned from this teaching?

What is one thing you can do to implement this teaching?

Faith Declaration:
I thank You Lord for giving me Your Word to renew my mind. I praise You for the help of Holy Spirit to bring my thoughts captive to the obedience of Christ and into conformity with Your Word and the Mind of Christ. I renounce the patterns of thought that have had negative impact on my life and on others, in Jesus' Name. Amen. I dedicate my mind to You, Lord and command it to focus on good, righteous, positive things and produce good fruit in and through my life, in Jesus' Name. So help me God, Amen.

6

How to have a Healthy Soul: *Tame Your Tongue; Move On; Serve Others*

Dear friend, I pray that you are doing well in every way and that you are healthy, just as your soul is healthy.
3 John 2 ISV

In the previous two chapters, I described three ways you can cultivate a healthy soul, namely, by becoming more like Jesus, by cultivating more joy in your life and by training your mind. In this chapter, I will outline the final three of the six ways, which are (i) Tame your tongue; (ii) Forgive others, be healed and move on; and (iii) Serve others.

(i) Tame your Tongue

Your words have power and they can do both harm and good. God wants you to use them for good, but the devil wants you to use them for harm. Believers who build enjoyable relationships and enduring ministries, harness the positive power of their tongue. Effective Christians learn to control their tongues and emotions.

> *The tongue has the power of life and death, ...*
> *Proverbs 18:21a*
>
> *A fool's mouth is his undoing and his lips are a snare to his soul.*
> *Proverbs 18:7*
>
> *..you have been trapped by what you said, ensnared by the words of your mouth*
> *Proverbs 6:2*

What we speak is a matter of our choice. God wants us to choose to speak for His glory and the blessing and benefit of people. He wants us to choose to not be a mouthpiece for the devil or this sinful world.

Speak for God's glory. Speak for the blessing and benefit of people, including yourself. Choose to not be a mouthpiece for the devil or this sinful world.

We will reap the consequences of how we choose to use our tongues.

> From the fruit of his lips a man is filled with good things as surely as the work of his hands rewards him.
>
> Proverbs 12:14

> The tongue of the wise brings healing
>
> Proverbs 12:18

Your tongue can bring healing or do harm to others and to yourself.

> The tongue also is a fire, a world of evil among the parts of the body. It corrupts the whole person, sets the whole course

> of his life on fire, and is itself set on fire by hell
>
> James 3:6

Your words not only affect other people and yourself, they also impact Holy Spirit.

> Do not let any unwholesome talk come out of your mouths, but only what is helpful for building others up according to their needs, that it may benefit those who listen. And do not grieve the Holy Spirit of God, ... Let there be no filthiness (obscenity, indecency) nor foolish and sinful (silly and corrupt) talk, nor coarse gesturing, which are not fitting or becoming: but instead voice your thankfulness [to God].
>
> Ephesians 4:29,30a NIV and 5:4 AMP.

Having a negative, complaining and critical tongue will sabotage not only your own potential and destiny, but also that of the other people who are damaged by your negative words. It will also ruin the quality of your life and relationships.

> Whoever would love life and see good days must keep his tongue from evil and his lips from deceitful speech.
>
> 1 Peter 3:10

(ii)   Forgive; Be Healed; Move On

I think it was Robert Schuller who first used the rhyming verbs in these two sentences: When somebody has hurt you, don't curse it and make it worse; don't nurse it inside and allow it to fester; and don't rehearse it to others who can't help you, so that you pollute and prejudice them, as well as yourself. Instead, disperse it to God in prayer and He will reverse it and work it for good.

Don't curse it, nurse it or rehearse it. Disperse it to God in prayer and He will reverse it.

After all my years in ministry, I have been hurt so many times, I can't even count the number of my scars. I have felt as if I was stabbed in the back, the heart, the head, the stomach and anywhere and everywhere else that it is possible for another person to cause me pain.

I remember one man who waited for a significant church meeting to start and then produced what he thought was evidence of my unsatisfactory leadership. I felt as if he just walked up to me with a knife, pierced me and twisted it to cause the maximum pain and embarrassment that he could. Time and the way I responded to what he did, proved him wrong. Sadly, he backslid after leaving our church.

Another man told people that it was his ministry to empty our church. Praise God, the Lord changed his heart. When I went to see him about his unacceptable behaviour and conversations with others, he had a literal covenant typed up for us both to sign. The covenant was his commitment to never be negative again concerning me or my ministry or the church I was pastoring. When he was reading a Christian book at work on his lunch break, the author used the very words I had said to him on the phone, just 24 hours earlier. He knew God was speaking to him and thankfully he was obedient to what the Lord had revealed in His Word and by His Spirit.

To have a healthy soul, we need to be merciful not judgemental. (Matthew 7:1-5). We need to forgive others. That is a condition of God forgiving us. (Mark 11:24-25). Through exercising mercy and forgiveness you will keep your heart free of poisonous grudges and heart-hardening resentments.

This means you don't keep thinking about the incident over and over. Don't keep complaining to others about how unfairly you were treated and how hurt you still are. How can you get healed if you keep the pain alive?

Instead, get the help you need and disperse your feelings about the situation and the justice of your case in prayer to the Lord. He has promised in Romans 8:28 to turn the situation around for your good ... provided you love Him and are called according to His purpose; in other words, you are doing what God wants you to do with your life.

I have learned that, according to Luke 6:27-28, when dealing with seriously hurtful issues, I have to bless my critics, my "enemies", before I get healed inside. I mean sincerely bless them, not ask God to hit them with a bolt of lightning or a taste of their own medicine. I must ask God to bless them, just as I would want Him to bless me or my friends. Every time I have done that, I have been fully, deeply and permanently healed inside.

In Hebrews 10:17, quoting Jeremiah 31:34, the Bible tells us that God remembers our sins no more. He doesn't develop amnesia. He simply shuts the door of His memory concerning our sins. We have to discipline ourselves to do the same in regard to both (a) sins we have committed but also confessed to the Lord that are washed away by the Blood of Jesus; and (b) sins, hurts and offences that have been committed by others against us.

Whether the person has deliberately or inadvertently hurt you, you must, like God does, both forgive the person and shut the door on the incident/s.

You need to learn to both forgive and forget, by shutting the doors of your mind and your mouth regarding the negative incident/s and the people involved

---

Let me quote what the Lord taught me from Jeremiah in the book of Lamentations. This is in my book "You Can Prophesy – Supernatural. Simple. Safe."

> *Because of the Lord's great love we are not consumed, for his compassions never fail. ^{23} They are new every morning; great is your faithfulness. ^{24} I say to myself, "The Lord is my portion; therefore I will wait for him."*
>
> *Lamentations 3:22-24*

"I had to learn, and am still learning, how to shut the door on the past when faced with difficult situations or negative circumstances. This may include the very recent past. Whether someone hurt you years ago or only yesterday, you must learn how to get over it. You can do this by exercising forgiveness, by getting over yourself, and by stepping into the Lord's new mercy, new grace, new love, new blessing, new hope and new power! God has provided these for you each and every day. This good habit, this good love relationship exchange will bring the Lord's victory, healing, peace and joy into your life."

You will also help yourself get healed when you take steps to move forward in your life. I am not saying that as soon as you have a relationship breakdown, you go and find somebody else. That is a recipe for more disaster.

Firstly, get your relationship with God right. Then use Godly wisdom and the enabling of Holy Spirit to rebuild your life inwardly and outwardly. The Lord will help you go forward in every area of your life, one step and one day at a time. God will restore all you have lost. You will experience a positive future, no matter how unlikely it seems when you are wrapped in pain. The time will come, as you stay the course with God, when the joy of the Lord will be your strength. (Nehemiah 8:10).

Secondly, do the natural things you can do to stabilise your emotions and the other areas of your life. I haven't got time in this chapter or book to go into the details of the five stages of grief made famous by Dr. Elizabeth Kubler-Ross, in her best-selling book *On Death and Dying* (1969), which pioneered people's understanding of this process. Although it was focussed on physical death, the five stages of grief are also experienced to some degree in other areas of life such as in a relationship breakup or through the loss of a job. The stages are: Denial; Anger; Bargaining; Depression; Acceptance.

You have to allow yourself time to go through the process of healing that is appropriate for you. It may take more time and be a different path of recovery than others. That doesn't matter. What does matter is that you get the help and take the time you need to get healthy inside. If your normal eating and sleeping patterns are disturbed, make sure you consult your doctor.

(iii) Serve Others

When I was born again and began to go to church regularly, my first pastor had a saying: "We are saved to serve."

In John chapter 15, Jesus taught us that it was in our new Christian DNA to bear fruit, which is the teaching of Paul in Ephesians 2:10.

This is to my Father's glory, that you bear much fruit, showing yourselves to be My disciples.

John 15:8

For we are God's handiwork, created in Christ Jesus to do good works, which God prepared in advance for us to do.

Ephesians 2:10

Some time ago I learned of a testimony told by Matthew Barnett, founder of the Dream Centre in Los Angeles. He said that a lady came to him for counselling for her depression. He spent some time with her and ended by saying he would not make a second appointment until she had spent a week serving in one of their community-oriented ministries. She never returned for further counselling, because she found a satisfying purpose for her life. She was both healed and uplifted by making a positive difference in other people's lives.

Serving others forces you to change your focus from yourself and your needs to God and His answers and to other people and the joy you can bring into their lives.

The fruit for God we are to bear is at least three-fold

(i) The fruit of character, of Godliness, of Christ-likeness, in other words the fruit of the Spirit. (Galatians 5:22-23);

(ii) The fruit of service or good works that are either or both practical and spiritual. (Matthew 5:16; Hebrews 13:16; John 14:12).

In order to bear the fruit of service, it is helpful to discover your own spiritual gifts and the other talents that God has given you which equip you to help and bless others. Rick Warren was the first to describe this process by means of a life and personality matrix he developed which he entitled using the acronym S.H.A.P.E. I added a "D" to the end of his acronym, as you can see from the following words. The matrix enables you to discern your destiny by examining your Spiritual gifts, Heart (passion; motivation), Abilities, Personality, Experiences and Dreams.

(iii) The fruit of spiritual reproduction, that is, winning people to Christ and helping them grow in the Lord. Jesus called this discipleship. (Matthew 28:19; 2 Timothy 2:2).

Conclusion from the prayer in 3 John 2

Your finances and your health matter to God; but the most important thing in your life is the health of your soul and the prosperity of your spiritual life. When you get your inner self healthy, the other areas of your life will improve.

What is one thing you have learned from this teaching?

What is one thing you can do to implement this teaching?

Faith Declaration:

I thank You Lord because where I am weak, You in me are strong. I dedicate my whole being, especially my mind and mouth, afresh to you today for righteousness sake, in Jesus' Name. Amen. I declare that with the help of Holy Spirit my words will edify others and glorify God. I forgive each and all who have hurt or offended me or my family, whether deliberately or innocently. I proclaim Your blessing over them and thank You for my healing. I declare that Your power is in me and Your grace upon me to do good to people in my life today, by natural and supernatural means, in Jesus' Name. Amen.

7

Essential Christian Qualities: *Love and Holiness*

And so faith, hope, love abide [faith — conviction and belief respecting man's relation to God and divine things; hope — joyful and confident expectation of eternal salvation; love — true affection for God and man, growing out of God's love for and in us], these three; but the greatest of these is love.

1 Corinthians 13:13 AMP

But you, man of God, flee from all this, and pursue righteousness, godliness, faith, love, endurance and gentleness.

1 Timothy 6:11

There are five essential qualities every Christian must consistently display if they are to fulfil their true potential and destiny in Christ. The five qualities are Faith, Hope, Love, Wisdom and Righteousness.

All of them are necessary, just as we need our head, our arms, our torso, our legs and our feet to be a complete person. Nevertheless, I am going to say something about each of the five in a particular order.

(i)　　　Love is pre-eminent, because God is Love

Love is given pre-eminence in 1 Corinthians 13:13, where the verse says it is the greatest of the three qualities mentioned, faith, hope and love. The primary reason love is pre-eminent is because the Bible says that "God is love." (1 John 4:8) It's not that God has love, He is love.

When you live by love, you live by the best of all values. You stick to what you believe and how the Bible says you should live, no matter what the devil, people and life throw at you.

When you live by love, you live by the best of all values and you stick with your values, no matter what.

(a) One method of living by love is by implementing the Golden Rule consistently in your decision making and lifestyle.

Do unto others, as you would have them do unto you
Luke 6:31

I have made literally thousands of small and big decisions in my life based on the Golden Rule. It may have been as simple as doing grandma's taxi run with the grandchildren, when my wife was too tired to keep her promise.

Sometimes it was a bigger issue, such as when our church had needs for our building fund at a time when we didn't have much finance. Another fairly local church also needed some building money. So, our church gave up a week's offerings to donate to them. This was not only a love principle, but a faith one, because we believed that as we sowed, so would we reap. God was faithful to us and so were the people who served the Lord with us. When I handed our church over to the next Senior Pastor, we had a debt free property and facilities worth close to three million dollars.

I have to add here that the Lord has a sneaky sense of humour. I say humour because the day we received our give-away offerings, they were bigger than we had received for a long time. I say sneaky because, God was checking whether we were people of our word. Would we give it all away, or would we keep some to meet our own needs. We passed that test and gave it all, unlike Ananias and Sapphira in Acts chapter 5. Sadly, it is also unlike some pastors I have heard of who take up an offering for a visiting minister but only give him a part of what is received.

(b) Another way of living the love life is by blessing people around you. Be an encourager of others, even if you feel as if you need some encouragement yourself. It is an amazing thing that happens time and time again: as you bless and encourage others, strength and joy flow back in to you.

(ii) Righteousness ranks second

My second-ranked quality is righteousness, otherwise known as holiness, integrity, morality, ethics and purity.

I rank this second for three reasons:

(a)   The Name of God's Holy Spirit.

God Himself chose the Name of the Third Person of the Trinity. He could have called Him Loving Spirit, or Grace Spirit, or Omnipotent Spirit or many other such titles. However, the quality of Holiness was so important to the Lord, that He included it in His Spirit's Name. This quality of the Divine character is so important in Heaven that angels repeat it over and over again: "Holy, Holy, Holy is the Lord God Almighty."

(b) God's love and holiness met at the cross.

God's love forced Him to find a way to exercise judgement over our sin and reclaim the authority over planet earth that Adam and Eve had surrendered to Satan, without hurting us.

God did not want to lose the relationship and partnership He created us to enjoy together. He did not want us to eternally forfeit our friendship with Him, nor our rights as His children to share in His inheritance and to partner with Him in His eternal, as well as His earthly, purposes.

So, Father God sent His Son Jesus to live a perfect life, to be punished for us and to triumph over Satan, sin, sickness and every negative and evil thing on our behalf.

I cannot help shouting Hallelujah right now and I urge you to do the same. How amazing it is, yes it is indeed amazing grace, to realise that Jesus came to get what we deserved, which was punishment for our sins, so that we could get what He deserves which is blessing forevermore.

(c) The seriousness of verses such as Hebrews 6:4–6; 10:26–31; 12:14.

> *This is how we know who the children of God are and who the children of the devil are: Anyone who does not do what is right is not a child of God.*
> *1 John 3:10*

John learned this from what Jesus said in Matthew 7:16-20: *"by their fruit you shall know them."*

It is not enough to know you are clothed with the righteousness of Christ. A true Christian lives righteously, in the practical realities of their daily lives.

> *Therefore, since we have these promises, dear friends, let us purify ourselves from everything that contaminates body and spirit, perfecting holiness out of reverence for God.*
> *2 Corinthians 7:1*

It is not possible to mix darkness with light. You must not live for God on Sunday and the devil the other days of the week. You cannot fool God by putting on a good, religious show in public and in church but live an ungodly, worldly, selfish life when you are out of the Christian spotlight. (Galatians 5:17-21; Hebrews 4:13).

Jesus saved His worst pronouncements for the hypocritical religious leaders of His day. There is nothing that stinks more to God than sin boiled together with religion.

To live with righteousness means living in integrity, in every area of your life. Be honest, be trustworthy. Be the same in private and in the dark as you are in church and in public. Be of good reputation. Don't cheat on your wife or in your exams.

To live with righteousness means living in integrity, in every area of your life

If you live a good and godly life, you won't have to worry about what people say behind your back, because you won't be giving them any ammunition.

That is not to suggest we will never be criticised. Criticism is inevitable and unavoidable. If people criticised the perfect life that Jesus lived, then other negative-minded people will criticise you today.

Keep reminding yourself that they have the problem, not you.

Be like the dog on the hunt, who doesn't stop to worry about his fleas. Keep pursuing the purpose of God for your life, which includes becoming more like Jesus and learning how to let Holy Spirit empower you to live a life that pleases God and blesses others.

Essential Christian Qualities: Love and Holiness

What is one thing you have learned from this teaching?

What is one thing you can do to implement this teaching?

Faith Declaration:

I thank You Lord that You love me so fully and faithfully and because You fill me with Your love, by Your Spirit. I know I could never earn or deserve Your love and You do not want or expect this. You have given me Your love so freely because of Your Son and Your grace. In Jesus' Name, I declare that by faith and with the help of Your Spirit I will live a life that demonstrates Your love to others. Lord, I am grateful that You consider me righteous in Christ and have clothed me in His righteousness. In Jesus' Name, I declare that by faith and by the power of Your Spirit I will live so that people see the fruit of Christian values and integrity in my life. Amen.

8

Essential Christian Qualities: *Faith, Wisdom and Hope*

But now faith, hope, love, abide these three; but the greatest of these is love.
1 Corinthians 13:13 NAS

In the previous chapter, I outlined the first two of the qualities Christians need to live a life that glorifies God and fulfils both their Divine potential and purpose. The qualities of love and holiness are part of the very character and essence of Who God is. Therefore they are essential to be manifested in the lives of people who are made in His image, as we are. The other three qualities outlined in this chapter are: Faith, Wisdom and Hope.

(iii)   The third of the five essential qualities of Christian living is Faith.

> *And without faith it is impossible to please God, because anyone who comes to Him must believe that He exists and that He rewards those who earnestly seek Him.*
>
> *Hebrews 11:6*

When we have faith in God and His Word and we use our faith, we will be rewarded by the Lord in this life and in the next.

All the promises of God are given to us to experience by grace through faith. With faith all things become possible, because there is nothing and no-one that is impossible to the Lord. Our faith empowers us to be His partners and activates His Senior Partnership in our lives.

The thing about faith is that it sometimes requires us to act beyond the understanding of our merely-human minds and to act by overruling our feelings; but we must always act in accordance with the principles of God's Word.

Living by faith means living according to God's Word. From time to time, this will require you to overrule your feelings and not rely on your merely-human understanding.

A great benefit of living by faith is that when you do what the Bible says, God does what the Bible says. For example, if you step out in faith and lay hands on the sick, God will start healing people through you. That is a great reward of faith.

One of the areas of life where too many Christians have difficulty putting their faith into action is in money management. The Lord has given us many promises regarding His rewarding those who handle their finances His way. Let me state it simply: to live by faith with your money, be a giver, not a taker. If you are going to be a taker at all, be a risk-taker for the glory of God.

By faith, be a giver, not a taker. If you are going to be a taker at all, be a risk-taker for the glory of God.

Every Christian should be committed to strengthening their faith in the specific areas in which they are weak. For example, if you are not sure the Lord is your provider, the only way to prove Him (and in Malachi 3:10 the Lord gives us His specific permission to do this, in this one area of believing His Word), is to adopt His financial principles on a consistent basis. He will demonstrate His faithfulness to you and to His Word. My wife and I have given the Lord the first 10% of our gross income as a tithe plus other giving for more than thirty years. He has never let us down and He never will. He has provided for all our needs and many desires and for all the ministry purposes He has given us to undertake with Him and for His glory.

(iv) The fourth essential quality in a Christian's life is Wisdom.

> *The beginning of Wisdom is: get Wisdom (skillful and godly Wisdom)! [For skillful and godly Wisdom is the principal thing.] And with all you have gotten, get understanding (discernment, comprehension, and interpretation).*
> *Proverbs 4:7 AMP*

> *The fool says in his heart there is no God.*
> *Psalm 14:1*

Hebrews 11:6 says we must believe that God exists. It is not enough to believe that some kind of God exists somewhere in the universe. We must believe that the God of the Bible exists and that He is as the Bible describes Him and that He acts in accordance with His Word. That is the kind of Faith which God rewards.

Recently, I had the opportunity to witness to the man who finished off the internal painting my wife Lynne had been doing over recent months. God touched him powerfully, causing his pain to subside and the strength in his elbow and forearm and wrist to increase. He felt the electric heat of the Holy Spirit touch him twice on two consecutive days, for which I praise God.

He said to me: "I have been doing a lot of thinking, but I just don't have the faith that you have." He added: "I believe in the universe." So, I talked to him about God being the only Un-caused Cause in the universe. I told him that it takes much more faith than I have to believe that banging a few rocks together, even for millions of years, could ever create anything that has life, such as a human being or a fish, a flower or a bird.

Living with divine wisdom means living by godly, Biblical principles. To do that, you cannot allow the world to be your teacher, nor let non-Christians shape the way you live.

Let me remind you that wisdom is the brother and co-worker of faith, not its enemy.

> *Wisdom is the brother and co-worker of faith, not its enemy.*

However, some people try to use wisdom as an excuse for unbelief! For example, if God told them to go to China to preach the gospel, they might say: "It's not wise for me to go. It's not the right time for my family, or that country is cracking down against Christians and my presence there would cause difficulties for the local believers." This is not how faith and wisdom interact.

Provided you have done your homework regarding knowing the Will of God, you go by faith. By this I mean that you have sought the Lord regarding His Will and you have checked with godly leaders about what you have been sensing is the Lord's Will. You don't go to China just because one person prophesied it; nor because when you were reading the newspaper (remember them?), it happened to open at a page where China Airlines was offering discounted flights.

Having properly and correctly discerned the Lord's Will, you don't tell the Lord it's not wise for you to go. Rather you ask for His Godly wisdom as to how and when you can go. He will show you how you can obey Him and do it by faith. This is how faith and godly wisdom work together.

(v) The fifth essential quality of Christian living is Hope.

The rubber hits the road with this quality when a loved one dies. The Bible has an answer with comfort for that.

> ... we want you to know what will happen to the believers who have died so you will not grieve like people who have no hope.
> *1 Thessalonians 4:13 NLT*

Biblical Hope is not wishy washy, daydreaming about things that are never going to happen. Biblical Hope is a confident expectation that something God has promised will surely come into the reality of your world even though it hasn't happened yet.

> *Hope that is seen is not hope at all. Who hopes for what they already have? ^{25} But if we look forward to something we don't yet have, we must wait patiently and confidently.*
> *Romans 8:24b (NIV)-25 (NLT)*

What Hope is

Hope is Future-oriented; Faith is Now.

Hope is God saying to Joshua: "Wherever your foot treads, I have given it to you."

Faith is Joshua stepping into the Promised Land and doing battle for what belonged to him, by Divine promise and authority.

Hope can be defined as something God has promised us that motivates us to act in ways which bring the things we are hoping for into reality in our lives. I believe that Hope inspires Faith. Faith grows in the garden of Hope.

If you can hope for something, if you can visualise it happening, you can begin to believe that it will happen. If you see it in God's word; if you can imagine that what God promises can become a reality in your life, then your faith will grow until it is strong enough to claim your Biblical inheritance.

The second meaning of Biblical hope is the vision or purpose to which God has called you. This definition of hope reminds and motivates us to get into alignment with our divine assignment. Put the purposes of God at the top of your to-do list, not at the bottom.

Hope is the soil in which faith grows. Hope motivates us to live according to God's promises and purposes

To live with hope is to be motivated to bring the promises and purposes of God into reality in and through your life and ministry. To live with hope is to live according to a God-given vision of His Divine purposes for your life.

Conclusion re 5 essential Christian Qualities

If a believer cultivates and operates in life according to these five Christian qualities, he will radiate the fragrance of Jesus. He will be effective in the Kingdom of God. He will live an exemplary and enjoyable and fruitful life that glorifies God and benefits people in his sphere of influence.

I encourage you to not allow the devil, people or any kind of circumstance, pressure, hurt or offence to cause you to waver from living your life according to these five essential Christian qualities: Love, Righteousness, Faith, Wisdom and Hope.

Healthy Soul: Faith Food Snack Pack

What is one thing you have learned from this teaching?

What is one thing you can do to implement this teaching?

Faith Declaration:

I thank You Lord for giving me the measure of faith I need to succeed in fulfilling my divine potential and destiny. Thank You for helping me grow in faith until all things become possible to me as they are to You. I thank you that my faith is sufficient for any and every situation I face, whether positive or negative, whether an opportunity or a challenge. I am grateful for Your wisdom. I declare that I have the mind of Christ and that as a son of God, I am led by Your Spirit. I praise You for giving me good, godly, wise people as counsellors, who help me make good decisions and keep me accountable to live by Your principles. I declare that I have confident expectation of Your promises coming to pass in my life. I decree that the purposes of God for my life will surely come to pass, in Jesus' Name. Amen.

9
24 hour Prayer
to Save a Multitude

Rescue others by snatching them from the flames of judgment.
Jude 1:23a NLT

Jesus answered him, "Truly I tell you, today you will be with Me in paradise."
Luke 23:43

According to current statistics, around 150,000 people die each day. That's nearly two people every second or every never-ending handclap. Whether young or old, rich or poor, male or female, educated or uneducated, overweight or underweight or in as good condition as a professional athlete, more than 100 human beings around the world will face their Maker every minute. That's over 6,000 per hour and more than 55 million per year. We Christians need to be praying for them to get saved before they meet the Lord face-to-face.

Just a few years ago in Victoria, a young 14-year old girl was picked up for a ride by a group of teenagers. She soon realised the driver was far too drunk to drive responsibly. They stopped at McDonalds to get some fast food. Unfortunately, she was not emotionally strong enough to refuse to get back in the car and then call her mum to come and pick her up. The group all piled back into the car. The drunk took the wheel and sped off. After a short time, the young girl sent her last text to a friend: "I'm afraid I am going to die." Sadly, a few minutes later, she did.

The two Scriptures at the beginning of this chapter tell us two things. Firstly, when the Lord answers this prayer, He spiritually snatches souls out of the very doors of Hell, out of the sulphurous snares of the devil. Secondly, when Jesus saved a thief on a cross near the end of his last day on earth, He gave us a Divine example of His willingness to save even criminals in their last hours.

A friend of mine came over from Western Australia to receive prayer at a large healing meeting in Brisbane. The night I took him there, thousands of people attended. They filled the huge auditorium. My friend got a touch from the Lord, but not a complete healing.

While I was praying for him that night, I began to intercede for everyone present who needed a healing. Holy Spirit said to me: "Why confine yourself to the walls of the building?"

That's when I began to pray lots of global prayers. I pray for souls and for revival in every nation. Based on the part of Lord's Prayer that says "Give us this day our daily bread", I also pray for the Lord to do many food and water miracles around the world. I ask Him to multiply food, to make dirty water clean and to provide streams in the desert. I call down rain as Elijah did. I pray that God will do these miracles in ways that bring Him glory, as well as meet human needs.

The greatest prayer the Lord showed me was based on the word "daily" in that same line of the Lord's Prayer. Holy Spirit led me to pray and ask as many Christians as I could influence to join me in this same prayer. That's why this chapter is included in my book.

The prayer is that people will hear the Gospel and respond to Christ in the last 24 hours of their life on earth. That includes the last 24 nano-seconds of their life.

Please pray with me that many people will be saved in the last 24 hours of their life on earth.

This could happen by any of three means: (a) a person, whether family, friend or stranger; (b) Christian media, such as a Bible, television, radio, a tract, a book, a CD, a DVD or an online teaching. This revelation is what inspired me to believe in the Kingdom power of the internet and Facebook and Christian television and radio; (c) a supernatural intervention of the Lord Himself, a Holy Spirit inspired vision or dream or the visit of an angel.

On one occasion Holy Spirit gave me this amazing glimpse into the day I walked into Heaven: An angel met me. He was going to take me to the Throne Room to meet my Heavenly Father, my Lord and Saviour, Jesus and my Helper, Holy Spirit. As I looked over to my right, I saw a massive crowd of people. They were just milling around until I turned to look at them. Suddenly they burst into exuberant praise to God and His Christ. They lifted up holy hands and praised with all their might. I asked the angel: "Who are they?" He replied: "They are the ones who were saved in answer to the prayer the Lord gave you to pray and to share with others."

So, when I heard the sad news report concerning the young girl to whom I referred above, I had the satisfaction of knowing that I had prayed for her salvation. I hope she is one of the crowd I saw praising the Lord in heaven.

I invite you to share in interceding for people like her by praying for people to be saved in their last 24 hours on earth.

I will add that I have subsequently extended my prayer to include people receiving Gospel revelation in their last 24 days and 24 weeks.

I extended the time-focus of my prayer because of the testimony of my dad. In the last months of his life, he loved me reading the Bible to him, especially the Parable of the Sower. However, for some reason, dad refused to give His life to Jesus, by praying the sinner's prayer. I couldn't understand why he was so enthusiastic for the Word, yet so reluctant to get saved.

I took my pastor along. He asked dad what was the reason for his reluctance. Because he didn't understand the Grace of God, dad said something like: "I am not worthy to be saved. I have made mistakes. I have sinned. I don't think I should cheat the system by getting saved so late in life."

My pastor shared the testimony of the thief on the cross next to Jesus. Dad was so impacted by that. He gave his heart to the Lord. On the night he died, Holy Spirit spoke to me through His Word, from Psalm 61 verse 7 in the King James Version. *"He shall abide before God forever."* I went to sleep in peace.

We sang that Psalm at dad's funeral, which was only a few weeks later.

Please pray with me that many people will be saved in their last 24 hours, 24 days or 24 weeks of life.

I believe in Bible verses that talk about household salvation (Genesis 6:18; Psalm 103:17; Isaiah 54:13; Jeremiah 32:38-41; Joel 2:28; Acts 2:38-39; Acts 16:31). The miracle of the Passover in Exodus chapter 12 is another type of household salvation. The blood of the sacrificed lamb protected the whole family inside the Israelite homes. The Egyptian children were not saved, because there was no blood of the lamb over their houses.

What is one thing you have learned from this teaching?

_____

What is one thing you can do to implement this teaching?

_____

Faith Declaration:

I praise You for sending Jesus to save us and rescue us from all the works of the devil. I thank You Lord because You can save people anywhere, anytime, no matter who they are or how far from You they are. I thank You for the promise of household salvation. I declare in Jesus' Name that my family will come to the Lord and many souls be saved during their last day on earth, in every nation. I speak prosperity to every Gospel-preaching person, church and ministry organisation on earth, in Jesus' Name. Amen.

ABOUT THE AUTHOR

Nick Watson has been happily married to Lynne since 1970. They have 3 children, Kylie, Simon and Rebekah; 4 (so far) grandchildren Katie, Rennick, Craig and Aiden; and 1 great-granddaughter, Riley.

Nick is the Founder, Principal Prophet, Author and Teacher, and People Builder of Prophetic Power Ministries.

He was for years the Senior Pastor of Bayside Christian Family (Apostolic) Church, a thriving Spirit-filled church in Brisbane, Queensland. Australia.

Nick has been a recognised prophet in the Apostolic Church Australia for more than 25 years. He has served in various denominational leadership roles.

Nick has preached and prophesied throughout Australia and overseas, with a signs-following ministry.

YOUR FEEDBACK

If this book "Healthy Soul: Faith Food Snack Pack" has encouraged your faith, please share your testimony with us at the email address below.

CONTACT Nick Watson

If you desire to contact Nick concerning a ministry engagement at your church, group, camp or leaders event please visit our website:

www.youcanprophesy.com

 www.facebook.com/nickjwatson.ycp

email: youcanprophesy@gmail.com

OTHER BOOKS by Nick Watson

Faith Food Snack Pack – Overcoming

Faith Food Snack Pack – Good News

Faith Food Snack Pack – Holy Spirit

Lessons From My Dog – 33 Faith Lifters

You Can Prophesy – Supernatural. Simple. Safe.

www.ingramcontent.com/pod-product-compliance
Lightning Source LLC
Chambersburg PA
CBHW072054290426
44110CB00014B/1681